Designs for Lamps I

Lampshade Designs

Charles Knapp

Pattern Editor

Charles Knapp

Photography

Judy Huffman
Randy Wardell

Project Fabrication

Charles Knapp

Typesetting and Layout

Randy Wardell

Printed in Canada

Published by

PUBLICATIONS INC

To receive our electronic newsletter or to send suggestions please contact us
by E-mail at: info@wardellpublications.com or visit our web site at: www.wardellpublications.com

Contents

Author Contact Information

Charles Knapp Studio,
RR#4 GB#413,
Huntsville ON, P1H 2J6 Canada
Ph: 705-789-8291

Notice: Due to variable conditions, materials and user skill levels, the publisher, author and material manufacturers disclaim any liability for adverse reaction, injury or loss resulting from the use of information in this publication.

Trade named tools and products, manufactured materials and/or proprietary processes mentioned or photographed for this publication are Trademarked™ and Copyrighted© by the respective manufacturers. All rights reserved.

Cataloguing in Publication Data

Knapp, Charles, 1949-
    Designs For Lamps I
    ISBN 0-919985-06-8

1. Lampshades, Glass - Patterns
2. Glass painting and Staining
3. Glass craft - Patterns
I. Title

NK 5440.L3 K63 1986 749'.63 C86-096597-3

Printed in Canada by Printcrafters Ltd.
Published simultaneously in Canada and USA
E-mail: info@wardellpublications.com
Website: www.wardellpublications.com

LAMP PATTERNS

Note: Lampbases are not available from Wardell Publications. Contact your local supplier.

PREFACE

The first time I held a piece of glass, a piece of blue opalescent, I thought it was the most beautiful thing I had ever seen. I went home and made a round leaded box out of it, and was thrilled. I still do that. When I find a new color, or a particularly striking sheet of glass, I go home and build it into something right away.

I have been a professional glass artist since 1974, and consequently do a lot of custom work. Some clients request that I design whatever I want, and some have very specific themes. Lamp design, for the most part, however, is free of outside influence. I choose a lamp base I like and design the shade as an extension of the base, so the shade and base become one lamp. It is very satisfying to take some glass I'm excited about and build it into a nice shape that lights up too! Please enjoy.

Charles Knapp

CONSTRUCTING A FOILED LAMPSHADE

Step 1: Trace pattern, making two copies, one on standard paper and one on card stock paper.

FIRST— Cut completely around the perimeter (outside) lines of the lamp pattern, following the center of each line.

SECOND— Cut the interior design lines following the center of each line. This will align each section to match the pattern above and below it.

Step 2: Carefully trace the pattern onto the glass using a felt-tip pen and cut the glass piece by scoring on the inside of the marker line. *You must always cut the line away* so the marker line is on the waste glass when you break it off. Check your glass piece with the pattern to verify that they are exactly the same size and shape. If the glass is not exact, you must grind it or cut it. Adjust your scoring to be more precise when scoring the next piece. Continue cutting your glass until all pieces are complete.

NOTE: When a pattern calls for Cut 1 Up 1 Down, you are required to trace and cut the glass with pattern facing you, **OVERTURN** pattern and trace and cut the glass with pattern facing down.

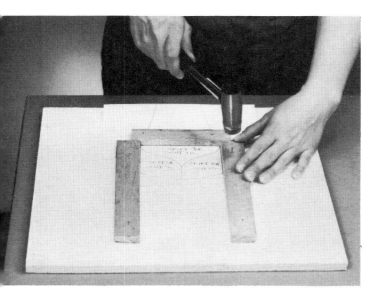

Step 3: When constructing a lamp that has panels with interior designs (a flat section containing two or more pieces), they must be fitted and assembled in a jig. Lay the working drawing (paper copy) of the pattern on your work table, face up. Nail three pieces of glazing lath onto your drawing so the outside line of the section to be assembled is half showing.

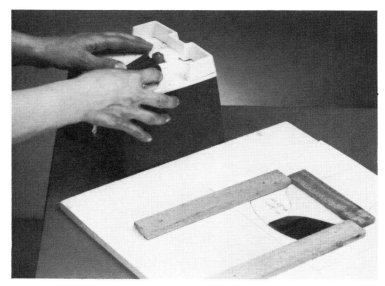

Step 4: Place one set of glass pieces into the jig as your drawing shows. If the pieces do not fit accurately, you will have to groze or grind them to fit or cut new ones. When the pieces fit into the jig correctly, clean each piece of glass and copper foil it.

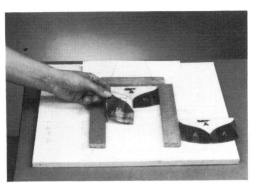

NOTE: If you intend to grind and fit all panel sets before foiling and assembling, you must code each set before removing them from the jig and keep the matched sets together.

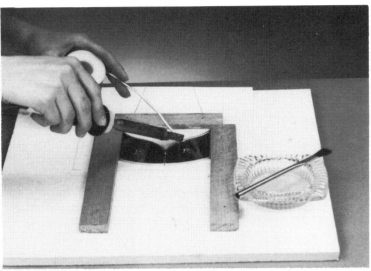

Step 5: Place the foiled glass pieces back into the jig and flat solder them. Remove the panel from the jig, turn it over and flat solder the other side. Finish by running a solder bead on the face side. Repeat for all panels.

Step 6: Start the lamp assembly with the row that is called the main body. This is the large section closest to the vase cap opening. Lay these pieces face side up on the work bench in a semi-circle. Use black plastic electrical tape (or in a pinch, masking tape) and tape the sections together. The areas where tape will come in contact with the glass *must be* clean or the tape will not adhere.

Step 7: Carefully raise this row up into a cone shape keeping the large diameter end on the bench. Bring the two adjoining side sections together and tape.

Step 8: You must be sure the bottom of the cone is *flat on* the bench. Flux and tack solder each seam at the bottom corner by applying a small dab of molten solder with the tip of your iron.

Step 9: Flux and solder completely around the top opening. Flat solder down the outside of each seam as best you can (leaving tape on) to strengthen the assembly.

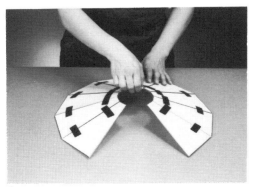 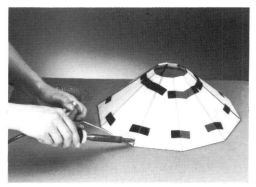 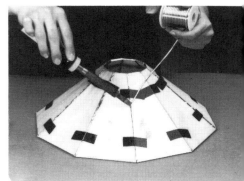

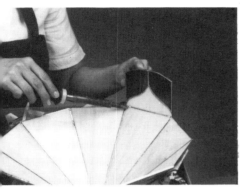

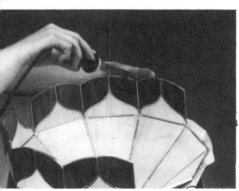

Step 10: *Important Step:* You have probably noticed how flimsy the lamp is at this stage. Attach the vase cap or spider now to strengthen its form. (see *Lamp Hanging Hardware,* Pages 9 & 10). The bottom must be sitting flat on the table when installing the vase cap to ensure the lamp has a proper shape. When the cap is soldered securely to the outside, carefully turn the lamp over and solder all inside seams and around the vase cap.

Step 11: Place your lamp upside down into a soldering box. (A cardboard box with newspapers loosely crumpled inside.) The assembly will continue by adding the panels of the next row (in the example shown it is the skirt or bottom row). Position and tack solder the first panel of this row to the main body.

Step 12: Place the second panel beside the first and tack it to the main body. Position pieces one and two until the seam meets evenly and tack solder together.

Step 13: Continue by adding the remaining panels in order around the lamp, tacking one to the other as you go. When the complete row is assembled, solder completely around the bottom edge. For more strength and stability, flat solder all the inside seams before moving on.

Step 14: Turn the lamp right side up in the soldering box. If you are constructing a lamp with a crown (upper most row) use the same procedure as described for the skirt assembly in Step 11, 12 & 13.

Step 15: The lamp should be completely assembled now and ready for final soldering. Remove all remaining tape. Position the lamp in the soldering box and level the seam you intend to solder (horizontal to the floor). Take your time and run a bead of solder. If the molten solder is flowing away from the seam or appears to be running downhill, this indicates the seam is not perfectly level. Reposition the lamp in the box and resume soldering.

HINT: If you are trying to fill a gap (a space between two foiled pieces), and the molten solder falls through, cover the space from the inside with masking tape to keep the solder from dripping.

Step 16: When you have completed soldering, do a quality check of all seams inside and out to make sure they are finished and uniform. Fine bead soldering is a difficult skill to master, don't be discouraged, remember practice makes perfect.

To finish your lamp, solder a wire around the bottom edge. For instruction and details see Page 11.

To clean your project of flux and solder residue use a glass cleaner, see Page 11.

To apply an antique patina to the solder beads (a coppery or black color), see Page 11.

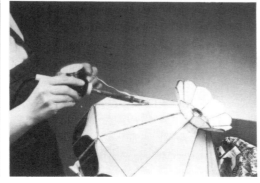

ALTERNATE LAMP ASSEMBLY METHOD

Instead of the row assembly described earlier, an alternative used by many crafters is a system called *row on row* assembly.

To use this method, substitute steps 11, 12, 13, & 14 in lamp assembly description.

Step 11: Place your lamp upside down into a soldering box. (A cardboard box with newspapers loosely crumpled inside as shown). The assembly will continue by adding the panels of the next row (in the example shown it is the skirt or bottom row). Lay these panels in sequence, side by side and face up on your bench. Tape them together in the same manner as you taped the main body. Gently lift the row on its edge, bend it around into a circle and tape the ends together. Tack solder all seams at top and bottom corners only.

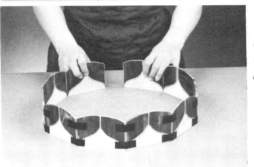

Step 12: Turn the main body section upside down into the soldering box. Gently lift the skirt section and place it on the main body. The seam corners of the two sections must line up one to the other. Tack solder the sections together at these corners.

Step 13: When the complete row is attached, solder completely around the bottom edge. For more strength and stability, flat solder all the inside seams before moving on.

Step 14: Turn the lamp right side up in the soldering box. If you are constructing a lamp with a crown (upper most row) use the same procedure as for the skirt assembly in Steps 11, 12, & 13.

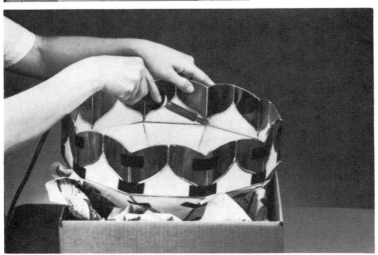

HANGING HARDWARE

Lamp Hanging Hardware: This is an integral part of a lampshade. It must be securely soldered to the top opening of a lampshade to solidify the structure and to provide hanging support for the electrical hardware. There are many different types of hanging hardware available, we will describe the two most common:

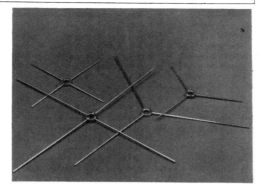

SPIDER

This is a brass ring about one inch in diameter with 3 or 4 arms radiating out from 6" to 12". The number of arms must divide evenly into the number of sides of your shade. For example, a six-sided shade requires a 3 arm spider while an eight-sided shade requires a 4 arm spider.

Installation:

Step 1: To ensure the spider hole is centered, measure the top opening of your lampshade and divide this dimension by two. For example, a 4" opening divided by two 2". Measure this distance from the center of the spider's central-hole down an arm and mark with a pen. Measure and mark all arms.

Step 2: Use a pair of pliers to bend the arms down at the marks. The angle of the bend must match the top angle of the lampshade. The first trial bend is simply a guess at the correct angle.

Step 3: Gently turn the lamp upside down and test the arm angles by positioning and centering the spider in the shade opening. Adjust the angles as needed. Each arm should extend approximately two to four inches from the top of the opening and straight down each seam, cut them shorter if necessary.

Step 4: When the spider fits the opening correctly, remove and tin each arm from the bend to the outside tip. Position and center the spider into the shade opening and solder the arms securely down the inside seams.

These are brass (or copper) disks which are available in various sizes. They car be plain or ventilated with fancy designs. The size must be matched to the shade top diameter.

INSTALLATION:

Step 1: To install a cap properly it should fit just inside the shade opening. Thi will ensure that it is soldered securely to the vertical seams of the lampshade. Vase caps are manufactured in standard sizes and often the shade opening is an odd size Most vase caps can be cut down with sheet metal shears to custom fit the opening

Step 2: If you were unable to find a cap to fit the shade opening exactly, choose a cap which is slightly larger than the opening. To mark the cap for trimming, place it on the shade opening from the outside and use a felt-tip pen to trace around the opening from the inside.

Step 3: Trim the cap following the traced line with sheet metal shears (tir snips). Place the cap back on the shade to check the fit and adjust as necessary

Step 4: The outside surface of the vase cap should be *tinned* with a thin layer o solder before installation. Tinning will allow antique patina (see Page 11) to colo the cap the same as the rest of the solder seams. It will also make soldering the cap to the shade easier.

NOTE: Since the vase cap draws heat away from the soldering area (referred to a heatsinking) it is more difficult to make the solder flow. To ensure a smooth finish more time will be required to heat both solder and metal while tinning.

Step 5: Position the cap on the shade opening and tack solder it. The cap must be centered and level on the shade. When the fit is correct, solder fully around the cap inside and out.

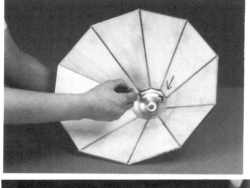

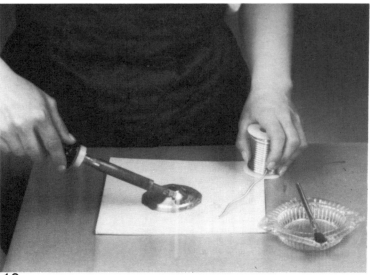

NOTE: If you are constructing a large shade, you can combine a cap and a spider for added strength.

WARNING: When wiring and installing your lamp you must consider all federal and local electrical codes and regulations.

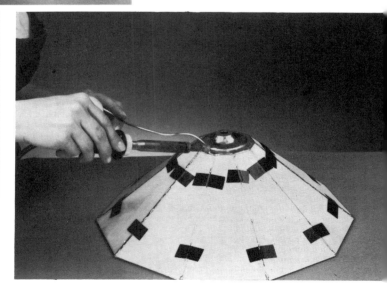

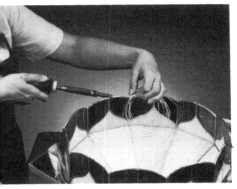

WIRE SUPPORT AROUND BOTTOM OF LAMP

It is recommended that a wire (14-gauge, brass or copper) be soldered around the bottom edge of your lamp for reinforcement. The wire will help to finish the bottom edge and holds it firmly together. Tack solder one piece of wire completely around the bottom edge and overlap the ends at least ½ inch. Finish the edge with a solder bead.

ANTIQUE PATINA

Best results are achieved when patina is applied to solder immediately after it is completed and cleaned with glass cleaner. Rub the solder using a soft rag or brush soaked with the liquid patina. Clean the solution from the glass immediately. Wear rubber gloves while handling this solution.

If your project has been finished for a few days, you must scrub down all the soldered seams with fine steel wool or a metal pot scrubber and clean to remove all corrosion before applying the patina.

CLEANING YOUR PROJECT

It is very important to clean your project as soon as you have finished working on it. If the flux is left on, it will corrode the solder even overnight. This will make touch-up soldering or final clean-up difficult. Any good quality glass cleaner will work, as will a solution of vinegar and water.

If the solder has corroded and is difficult to solder they can be cleaned by scrubbing with fine steel wool or a small wire brush. **Caution:** If you have already applied antique patina to the solder, scrubbing will remove it.

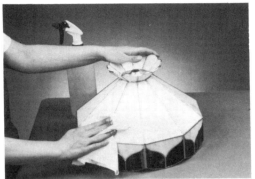

POLISHING OR WAXING

To preserve the shiny finish on the solder after a patina has been applied, use a good quality spray furniture polish. Apply the polish and rub all solder seams vigorously. For an even shinier finish, polish the patina with a jeweler's rouge cloth or use a brass or silver polish. Finish with an application of car wax. You can even polish the wax with a power car polisher.

PHOTOCOPYING YOUR PATTERNS

In recent years the photocopier has come into very wide use for many applications. Local copy centers are opening everywhere, offering services that include enlarging and reducing your originals. This opens up a multitude of possibilities for the stained glass crafter to alter the size of patterns quickly and easily. Enlarging is especially useful for free-form projects such as sun catchers or small panels due to the limitation in size, depending on the photocopier used.

There is, however, one note of caution concerning the use of photocopiers (other than possible copyright infringement). Most photocopiers do not make exact copies of the original. While the copy is very close, the mechanics of the copying process introduces some amount of distortion that can be disastrous when constructing a three-dimensional project such as a lampshade. The distortion usually results in a slight enlargement (or reduction) of the pattern in the vertical dimension to a greater degree than in the horizontal dimension. This does not mean you cannot use a photocopier for your lamp patterns, but it does mean you must carefully measure each pattern component to verify that they will fit one to the other.

Mushroom

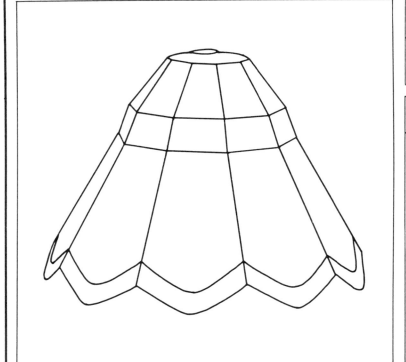

DEGREE OF DIFFICULTY

1	2	3	4	5

LAMPBASE INFO:

Name & Code #	Prestige # P088
Base Height—	5" (12.5 cm)
Harp Size—	4" (10 cm)

SPECIFICATIONS

# pieces—	36
# sides—	9
Bottom Diameter	6½" (16.5 cm)
Top Diameter	1¾" (4.5 cm)
Shade Height—	4¾" (12 cm)
Height (inc. base)—	9" (23 cm)
Vase Cap—	2" (5 cm)

MATERIALS

□ — ¾ sq. ft. Streaky Reddish Amber Opal (Background)

▨ — 1/3 sq. ft. Amber Cathedral (Top & Bottom Trim)

PROJECT INFORMATION:

A Hint: When selecting glass for the bottom trim, pick an easy cutting glass. The top opening requires a 2" (5 cm) vase cap, cut to fit the top diameter as shown on page 10.

Project 1　　MUSHROOM

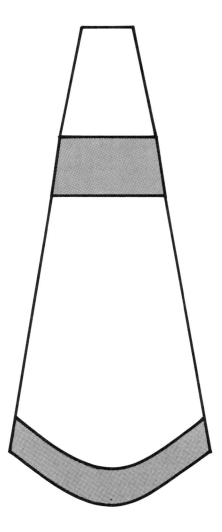

Cut 9 of Each

Tear Drop

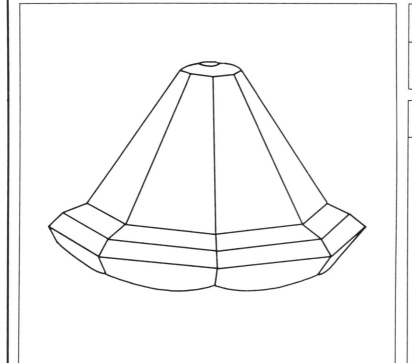

Project 2

DEGREE OF DIFFICULTY

1	2	3	4	5

LAMPBASE INFO:

Name & Code #	Roman # P086
Base Height—	5" (12.5 cm)
Harp Size—	3½" (9 cm)

SPECIFICATIONS

# pieces—	32
# sides—	8
Bottom Diameter	5" (12.5 cm)
Top Diameter	1 1/4" (3 cm)
Shade Height—	4" (10 cm)
Height (inc. base)—	9" (23 cm)
Vase Cap—	1½" (4 cm)

MATERIALS

□ — 2/3 sq. ft. Blue Opal (Background)

▨ — small piece Blue Cathedral (Trim Band)

PROJECT INFORMATION:
Note: Bottom skirt row will angle inward. The top opening requires a 1½" (4 cm) vase cap, cut to fit the top diameter as shown on page 10.

Project 2   TEAR DROP

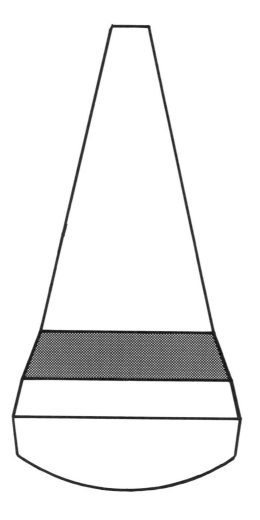

Cut 8 of Each

Corinth

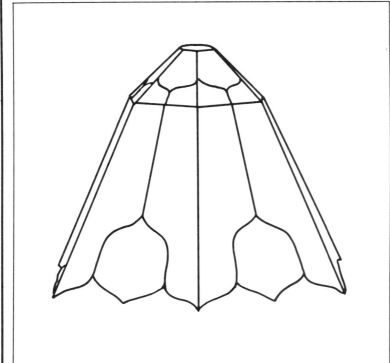

DEGREE OF DIFFICULTY

1	2	3	4	5

LAMPBASE INFO:

Name & Code #	Prestige # P085
Base Height—	5½" (14 cm)
Harp Size—	3½" (9 cm)

SPECIFICATIONS

# pieces—	36
# sides—	6
Bottom Diameter	5½" (14 cm)
Top Diameter	½" (1.25 cm)
Shade Height—	4½" (11.5 cm)
Height (inc. base)—	9" (23 cm)
Vase Cap—	not required

MATERIALS

— ¾ sq. ft.
Beige Opal (Background)

— small piece
Red Cathedral (Top Trim)

— small piece
Amber Cathedral
(Bottom Trim)

PROJECT INFORMATION:

No vase cap or spider is required for the top diameter. A solder bead around the opening's edge supports the lamp.

Project 3   CORINTH

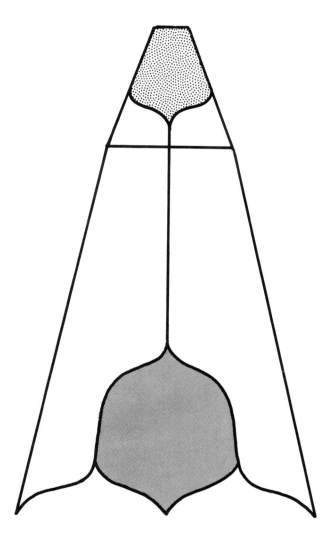

Cut 6 of Each

Classic

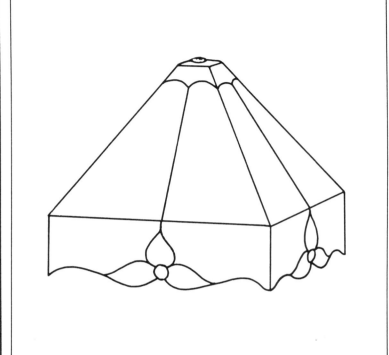

DEGREE OF DIFFICULTY

1	2	3	4	5

LAMPBASE INFO:

Name & Code # — Plaza # P084

Base Height— 5" (12.5 cm)

Harp Size— 4" (10 cm)

SPECIFICATIONS

# pieces—	36
# sides—	4
Bottom Diameter	5" (12.5 cm)
Top Diameter	1" (2.5 cm)
Shade Height—	5" (12.5 cm)
Height (inc. base)—	9" (23 cm)
Vase Cap—	1½" (4 cm)

MATERIALS

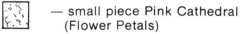

☐ — 1 sq. ft. Blue/Mauve Opal (Background)

▦ — small piece Blue Cathedral (Top Trim & Flower Center)

▢ — small piece Pink Cathedral (Flower Petals)

PROJECT INFORMATION:

The top opening requires a 1½" (4 cm) vase cap, cut to fit the top diameter as shown on page 10.

Project 4   CLASSIC

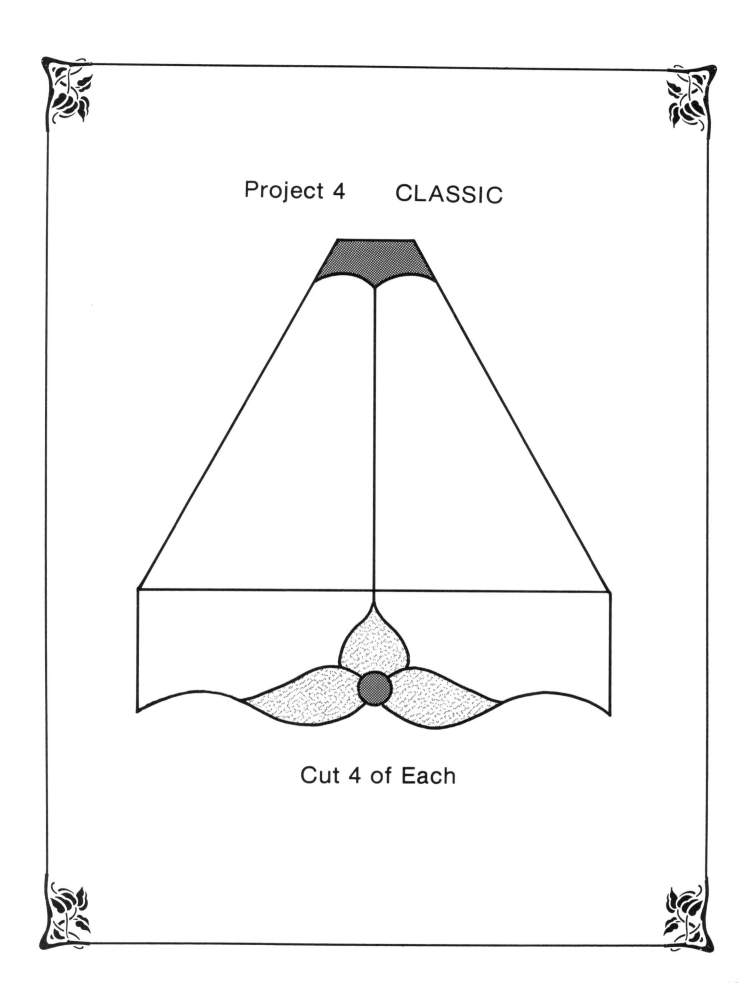

Cut 4 of Each

Mini Dome

Project 5

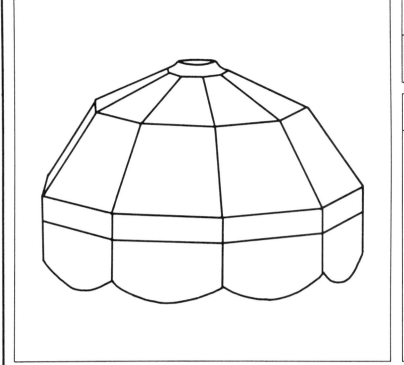

DEGREE OF DIFFICULTY

1	2	3	4	5

LAMPBASE INFO:

Name & Code #	Delta # P088
Base Height—	5" (12.5 cm)
Harp Size—	4" (10 cm)

SPECIFICATIONS

# pieces—	36
# sides—	9
Bottom Diameter	6" (15 cm)
Top Diameter	1" (2.5 cm)
Shade Height—	4" (10 cm)
Height (inc. base)—	9" (23 cm)
Vase Cap—	1½" (4 cm)

MATERIALS

□ — 2/3 sq. ft. Orange/White Opal (Background)

▤ — small piece Orange Cathedral (Trim Band)

PROJECT INFORMATION:
Note: To make assembly easier, start with second row from the top. The top opening requires a 1½" (4 cm) vase cap, cut to fit the top diameter as shown on page 10.

Project 5   MINI DOME

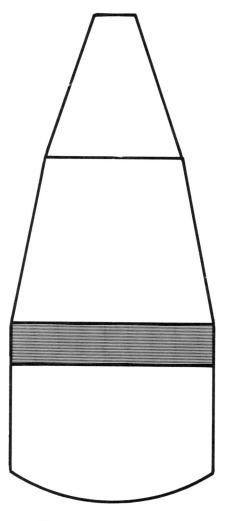

Cut 9 of Each

Super Dome

Project 6

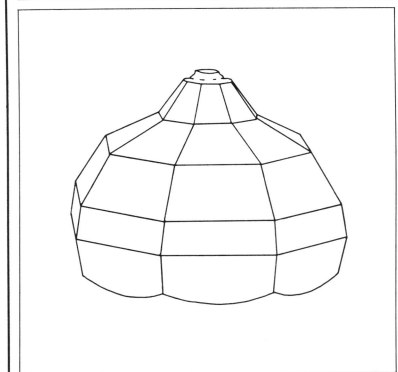

DEGREE OF DIFFICULTY

1	2	3	4	5

LAMPBASE INFO:

Name & Code #	Pavillion # P083
Base Height—	5½" (14 cm)
Harp Size—	4" (10 cm)

SPECIFICATIONS

# pieces—	40
# sides—	8
Bottom Diameter	6½" (16.5 cm)
Top Diameter	1" (2.5 cm)
Shade Height—	5" (12.5 cm)
Height (inc. base)—	9½" (24 cm)
Vase Cap—	1½" (4 cm)

MATERIALS

— ¾ sq. ft. White Opal (Background)

— 1/4 sq. ft. Irridescent Red (Trim Band)

PROJECT INFORMATION:
   Note: To make assembly easier, start with the second row from the top. The top opening requires a 1½" (4 cm) vase cap, cut to fit the top diameter as shown on page 10.

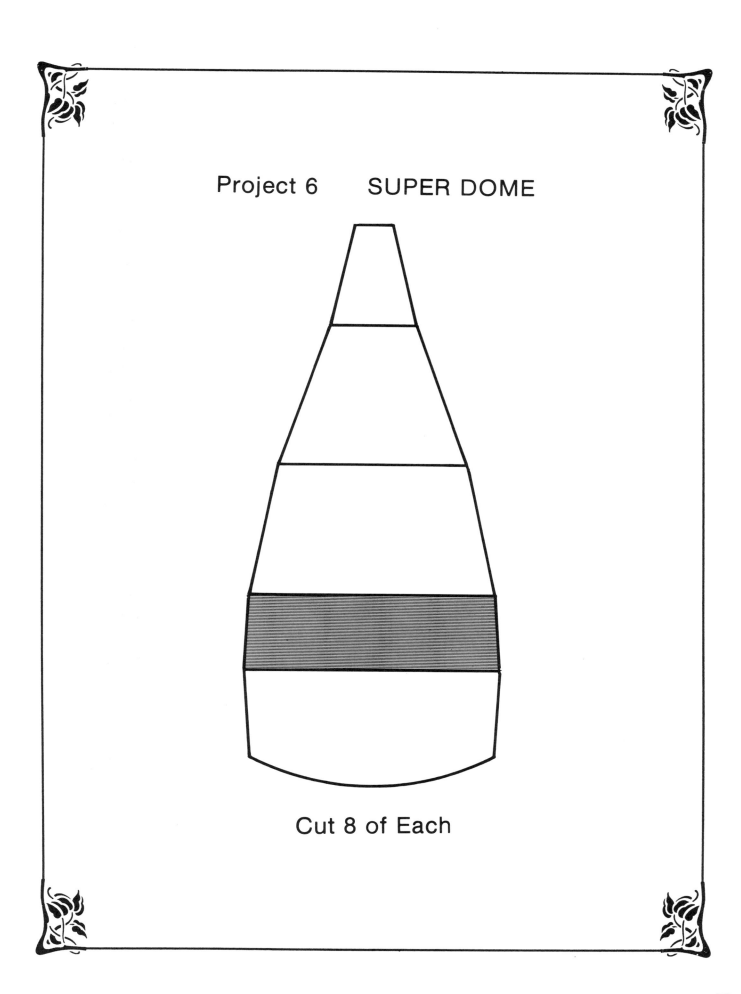

Project 6   SUPER DOME

Cut 8 of Each

Southern Bell

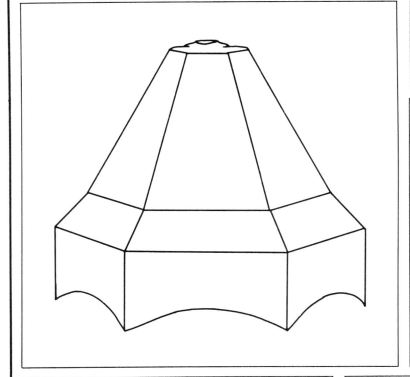

DEGREE OF DIFFICULTY

1	2	3	4	5

LAMPBASE INFO:

Name & Code #	Mini Flare # P037
Base Height—	5" (12.5 cm)
Harp Size—	6½" (16.5 cm)

SPECIFICATIONS

# pieces—	18
# sides—	6
Bottom Diameter	7½" (19 cm)
Top Diameter	2" (5 cm)
Shade Height—	7" (18 cm)
Height (inc. base)—	11½" (29 cm)
Vase Cap—	2½" (6 cm)

MATERIALS

— 1 sq. ft. Streaky Brown in White Opal (Background)

— 1/4 sq. ft. Streaky Green/Brown Cathedral (Trim Band)

PROJECT INFORMATION:
The top opening requires a 2½" (6 cm) vase cap, cut to fit the top diameter as shown on page 10.

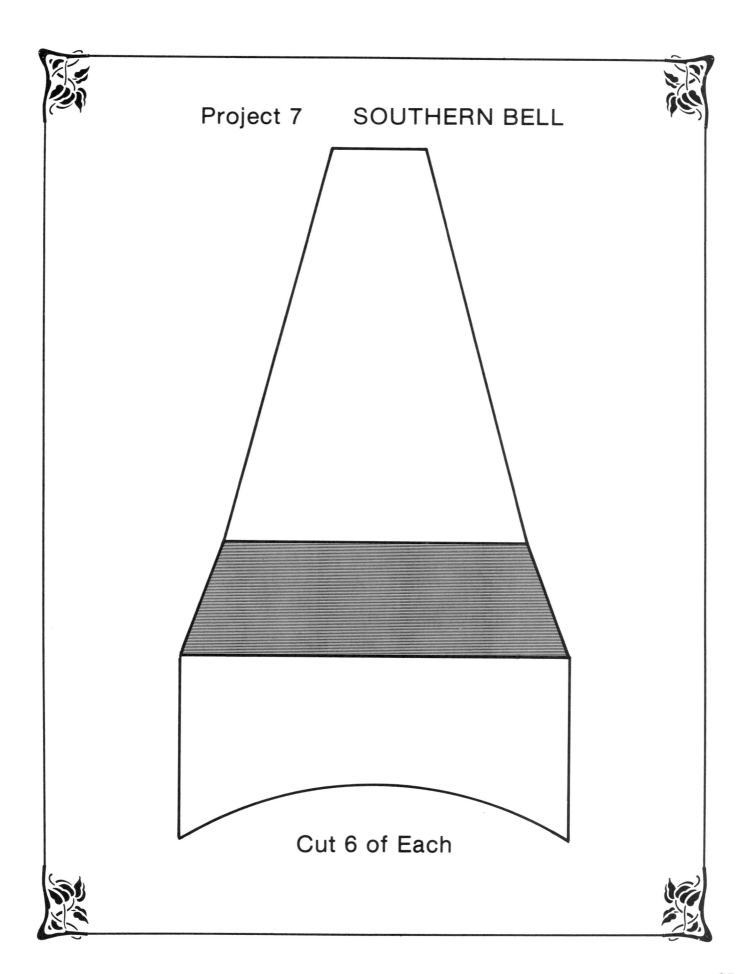

Project 7   SOUTHERN BELL

Cut 6 of Each

Ribbons

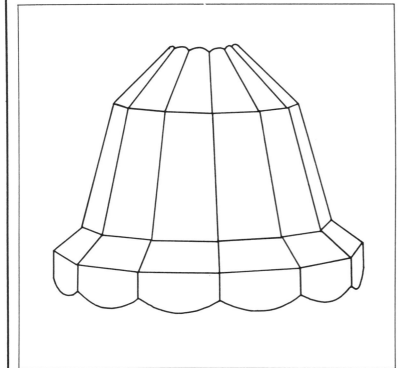

Project 8

DEGREE OF DIFFICULTY

1	2	3	4	5

LAMPBASE INFO:

Name & Code #	Mini Trumpet # P031
Base Height—	5" (12.5 cm)
Harp Size—	6½" (16.5 cm)

SPECIFICATIONS

# pieces—	48
# sides—	12
Bottom Diameter	8" (20 cm)
Top Diameter	1¾" (4.5 cm)
Shade Height—	6½" (16.5 cm)
Height (inc. base)—	12" (30.5 cm)
Spider— 1- 3 way	

MATERIALS

☐ — 2/3 sq. ft. of EACH
Blue Opal
alternated with
Streaky Pink Opal

PROJECT INFORMATION:

The top opening requires a 3-way spider. For installation technique, see page 9.

Project 8   RIBBONS

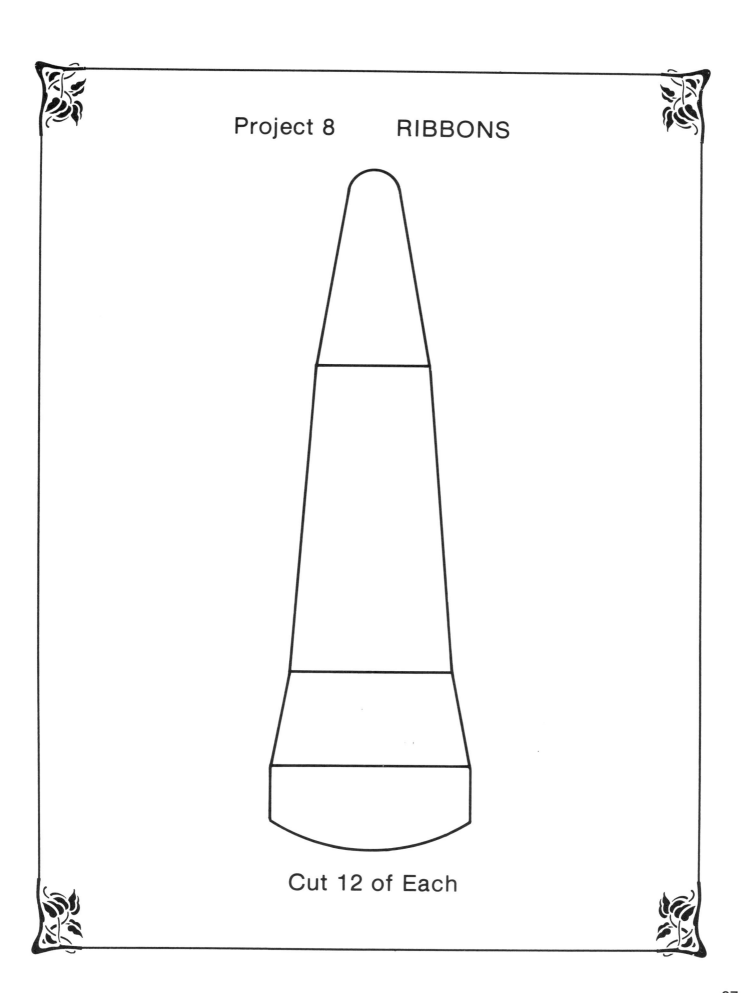

Cut 12 of Each

Tassels

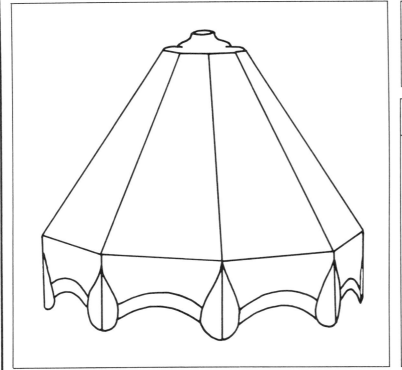

Project 9

DEGREE OF DIFFICULTY

1	2	3	4	5

LAMPBASE INFO:

Name & Code #   Tower II
                       # P028

Base Height—   7½" (19 cm)

Harp Size—   6½" (16.5 cm)

SPECIFICATIONS

# pieces—	40
# sides—	8
Bottom Diameter	8" (20.5 cm)
Top Diameter	2" (5 cm)
Shade Height—	7" (18 cm)
Height (inc. base)—	14" (35.5 cm)
Vase Cap—	2½" (6 cm)

MATERIALS

☐ — 1¾ sq. ft. Streaky Purple/Blue in White Opal (Background)

▨ — 1/4 sq. ft. Blue Cathedral (Bottom Trim Band)

▢ — 1/3 sq. ft. Purple Cathedral (Tassels)

PROJECT INFORMATION:

The top opening requires a 2½" (6 cm) vase cap, cut to fit the top diameter as shown on page 10.

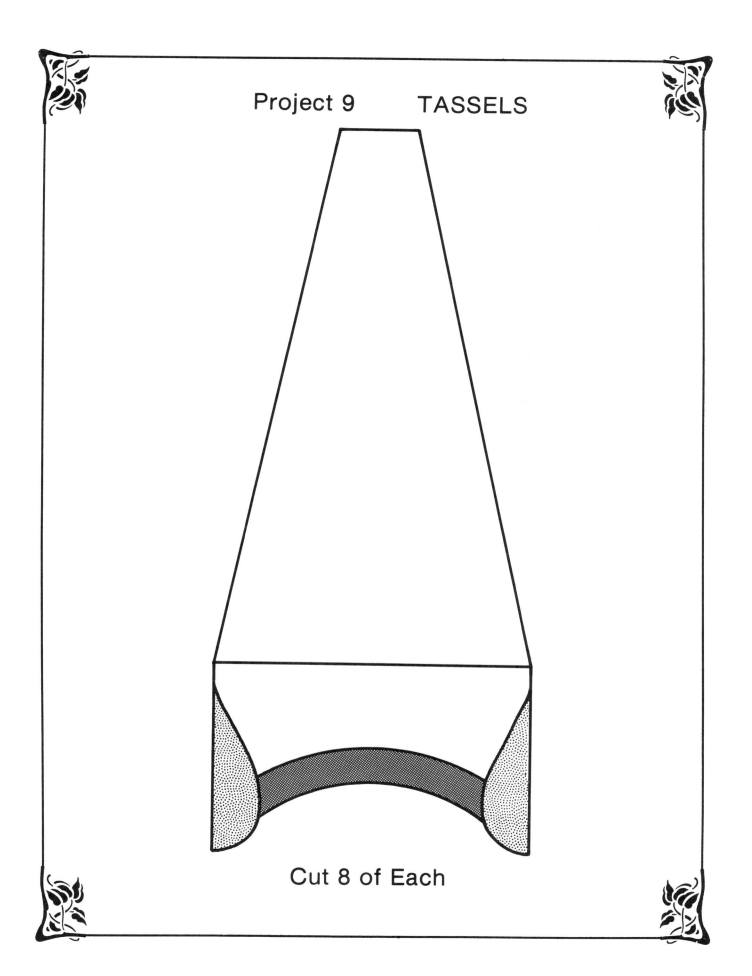

Project 9   TASSELS

Cut 8 of Each

Iris

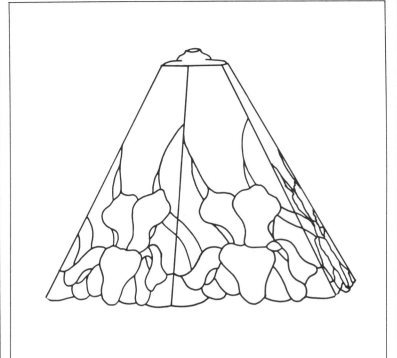

DEGREE OF DIFFICULTY

1	2	3	4	5

LAMPBASE INFO:

Name & Code #	Twisted Vine # P041
Base Height—	7½" (19 cm)
Harp Size—	6½" (16.5 cm)

SPECIFICATIONS

# pieces—	150
# sides—	6
Bottom Diameter	9½" (24 cm)
Top Diameter	2" (5 cm)
Shade Height—	7½" (19 cm)
Height (inc. base)—	14" (35.5 cm)
Vase Cap—	2½" (6 cm)

MATERIALS

- — 1¾ sq. ft. Blue/Purple Opal (Background)
- — ¾ sq. ft. Streaky Yellow Opal (Flower Petals)
- — small piece Yellow Cathedral (Underside of Petals)
- — small piece Green Cathedral (Leaves)

PROJECT INFORMATION:

The top opening requires a 2½" (6 cm) vase cap, cut to fit the top diameter as shown on page 10.

Due to the top angle of the lamp shade, a ½" (1.25 cm) riser on the harp or a flat vase cap is required to make allowance for lampbase harp.

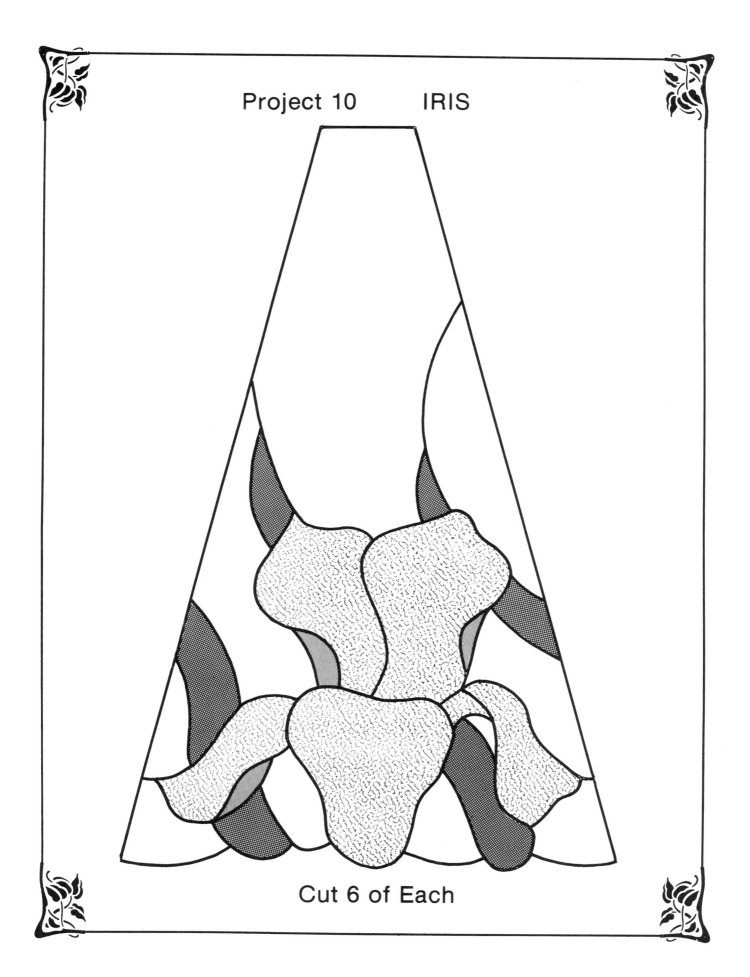

Project 10   IRIS

Cut 6 of Each

31

Flower Blossom Cone

Project 11

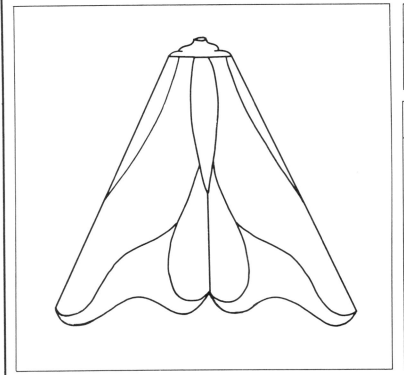

DEGREE OF DIFFICULTY

1	2	3	4	5

LAMPBASE INFO:

Name & Code #	Twisted Vine # P041
Base Height—	7½" (19 cm)
Harp Size—	6½" (16.5 cm) with a 1½" riser

SPECIFICATIONS

# pieces—	24
# sides—	6
Bottom Diameter	10" (25.5 cm)
Top Diameter	2" (5 cm)
Shade Height—	9" (23 cm)
Height (inc. base)—	15" (38 cm)
Vase Cap—	2" (5 cm)

MATERIALS

- ☐ — 2 sq. ft. Lt. Mauve Opal (Background)
- ▨ — 1 sq. ft. Dark Purple Cathedral (Bottom Trim)
- ▨ — 1/3 sq. ft. Green/Turquoise Opal (Joiner Pieces)

PROJECT INFORMATION:

Assemble panels of lamp together, one by one, add vase cap, then install joiner pieces.

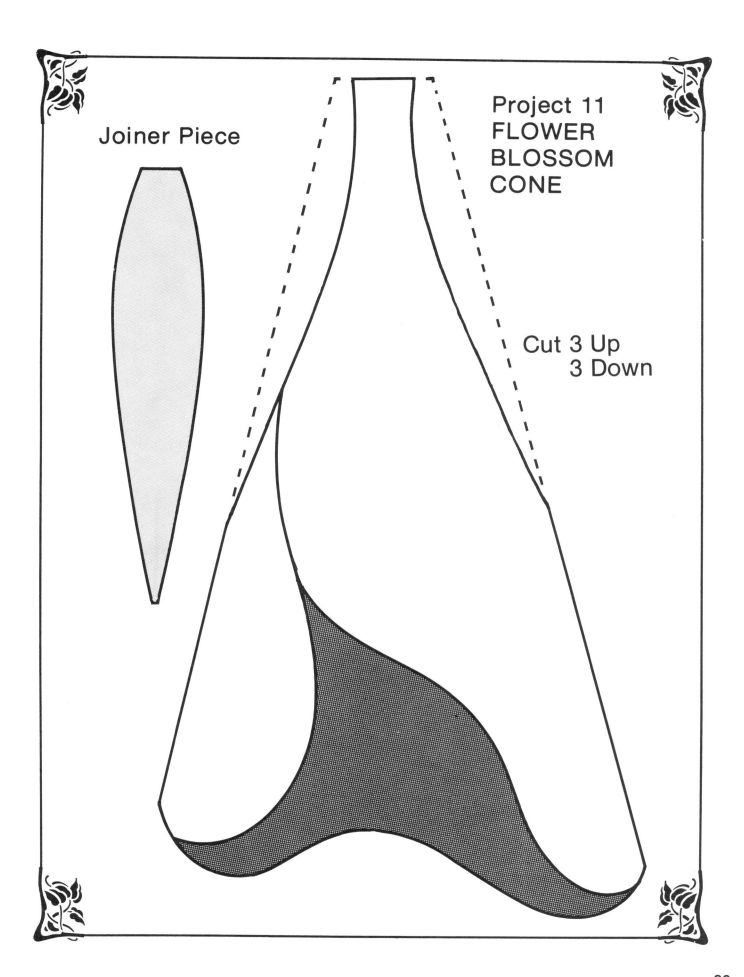

Joiner Piece

Project 11
FLOWER
BLOSSOM
CONE

Cut 3 Up
3 Down

Huntsville Cone

Project 12

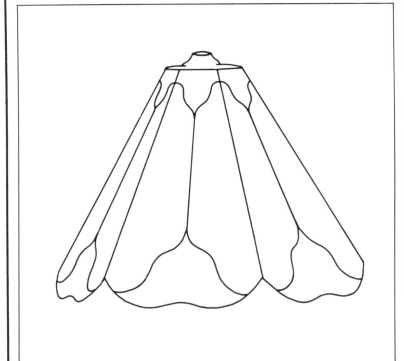

DEGREE OF DIFFICULTY

1	2	3	4	5

LAMPBASE INFO:

Name	Brass Spindle
Base Height—	8½" (21.5 cm)
Harp Size—	8" (20.5 cm)

SPECIFICATIONS

# pieces—	24
# sides—	6
Bottom Diameter	10½" (27 cm)
Top Diameter	2½" (6 cm)
Shade Height—	8½" (21.5 cm)
Height (inc. base)—	16" (41 cm)
Vase Cap—	3" (7.5 cm)

MATERIALS

☐ — 2 sq. ft. Streaky Blue/Mauve Opal (Background)

▤ — 1/4 sq. ft. Dk. Antique Purple Cathedral (Top Trim)

▦ — ¾ sq. ft. Streaky Purple/Amber Cathedral (Bottom Trim)

PROJECT INFORMATION:

A Hint: When selecting glass for the bottom trim, pick an easy cutting glass. The top opening requires a 3" (7.5 cm) vase cap, cut to fit the top diameter as shown on page 10.

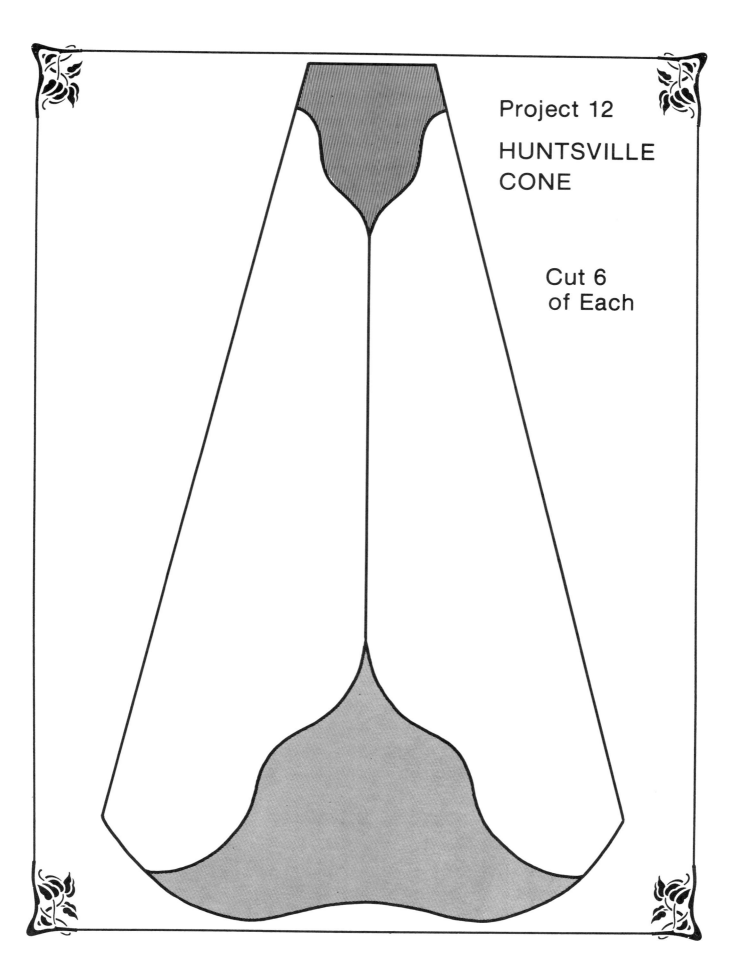

Project 12

HUNTSVILLE
CONE

Cut 6
of Each

Sea Cone	Project 13

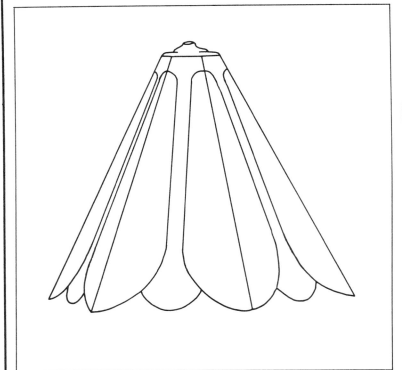

DEGREE OF DIFFICULTY

1	2	3	4	5

LAMPBASE INFO:

Name	Brass Classic
Base Height—	9" (23 cm)
Harp Size—	8½" (21.5 cm) and a 1" riser

SPECIFICATIONS

# pieces—	18
# sides—	6
Bottom Diameter	11" (28 cm)
Top Diameter	2" (5 cm)
Shade Height—	11" (28 cm)
Height (inc. base)—	18½" (47 cm)
Vase Cap—	2½" (6 cm)

MATERIALS

— 2 1/4 sq. ft. Strky Blue/Green Opal (Background)

— 1½ sq. ft. Streaky Rippled Blue Opal (Trim)

PROJECT INFORMATION:

To conserve your glass, lay the patterns beside one another, straight edge to straight edge. This lampshade is suitable for both swag or lampbase.

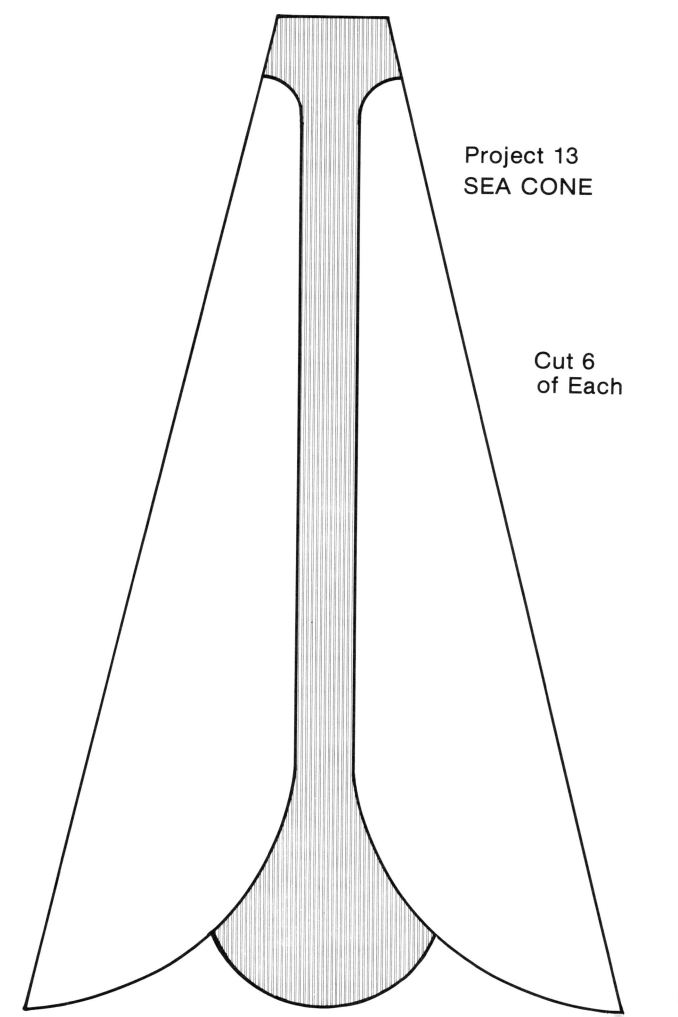

Project 13
SEA CONE

Cut 6
of Each

37

Ruby

Project 14

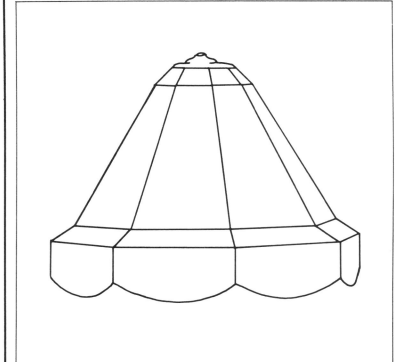

DEGREE OF DIFFICULTY

1	2	3	4	5

LAMPBASE INFO:

Name	Brass Classic
Base Height—	13½" (34 cm)
Harp Size—	9" (23 cm)

SPECIFICATIONS

# pieces—	32
# sides—	8
Bottom Diameter	12¾" (32 cm)
Top Diameter	2½" (6 cm)
Shade Height—	10" (25.5 cm)
Height (inc. base)—	22½" (57 cm)
Vase Cap—	3" (7.5 cm)

MATERIALS

☐ — 2½ sq. ft. Streaky Gray Opal (Background)

▨ — 2/3 sq. ft. Red Cathedral (Trim Top and Band)

PROJECT INFORMATION:
The top opening requires a 3" (7.5 cm) vase cap, cut to fit the top diameter as shown on page 10. This lampshade is suitable for both swag or lampbase.

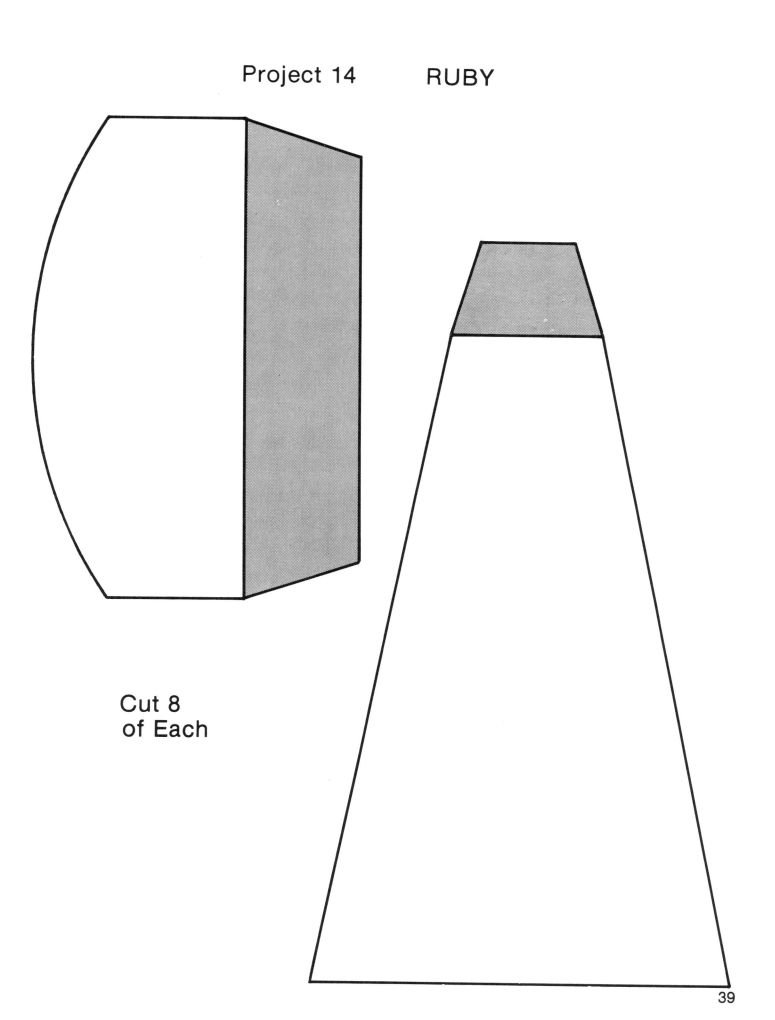

Project 14   RUBY

Cut 8
of Each

Bells	Project 15

DEGREE OF DIFFICULTY

1	2	3	4	5

SPECIFICATIONS

# pieces—	40
# sides—	8
Bottom Diameter	13"
	(33 cm)
Top Diameter	2¾"
	(7 cm)
Shade Height—	10½"
	(27 cm)
Vase Cap—	3"
	(7.5 cm)

Lampbase Info:

Base Height—	13½"
	(34 cm)
Harp—	8"
(20.5 cm) with a ½" riser	

MATERIALS

— 3 sq. ft. Streaky White Opal (Background)

— ¾ sq. ft. Streaky Green White (Trim Band)

— 1/4 sq. ft. Streaky Pink (Bell Shapes)

PROJECT INFORMATION: The top opening requires a 3" (7.5 cm) vase cap, cut to fit the top diameter as shown on page 10. This lamp is suitable for either swag or base.

Project 15   BELLS

Cut 8 of Each

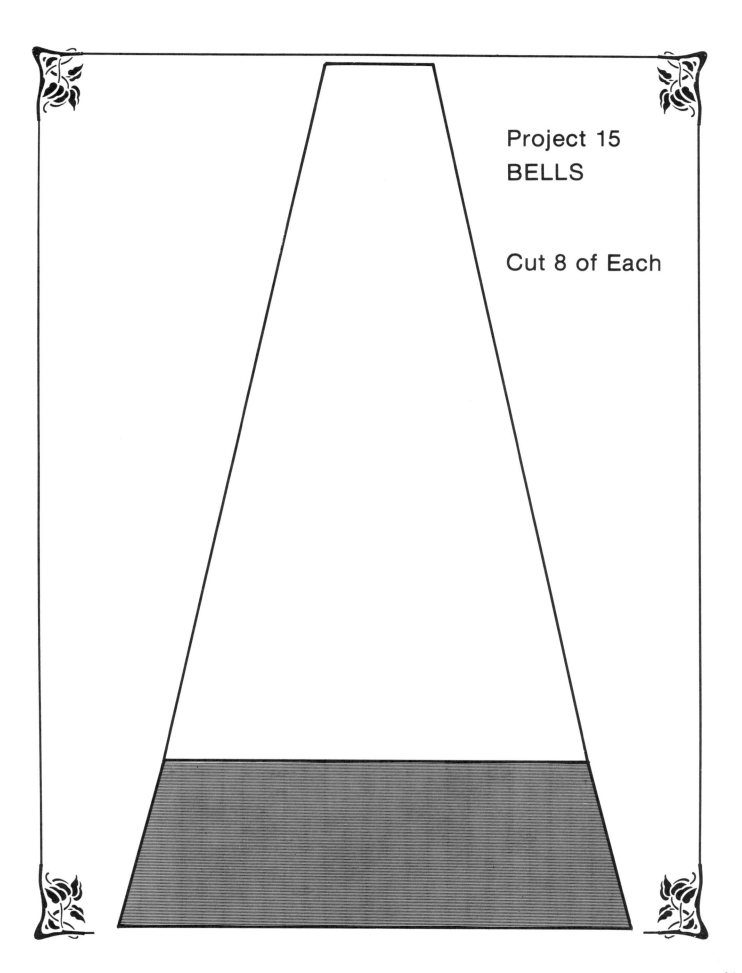

Project 15
BELLS

Cut 8 of Each

Floating Flowers  Project 16

DEGREE OF DIFFICULTY

1	2	3	4	5

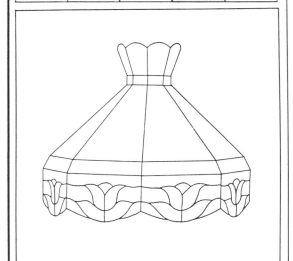

SPECIFICATIONS

# pieces—	112
# sides—	8
Bottom Diameter	15"
	(38 cm)
Top Diameter	3"
	(7.5 cm)
Shade Height—	14"
	(35.5 cm)
Spider—	1- 4 way

Lampbase Info:

Base Height—	13½"
	(34 cm)
Harp—	9"
	(23 cm)

MATERIALS

— 4 sq. ft.
Lt. Blue Opal
(Background)

— ¾ sq. ft.
Streaky Lavender
(Trim Band &
Leaf shapes)

— ¾ sq. ft.
Streaky Pink
(Collar & Flower)

PROJECT INFORMATION:
This lampshade is suitable for both swag or lampbase.

Project 16   FLOATING FLOWER

Cut 8 of Each

42

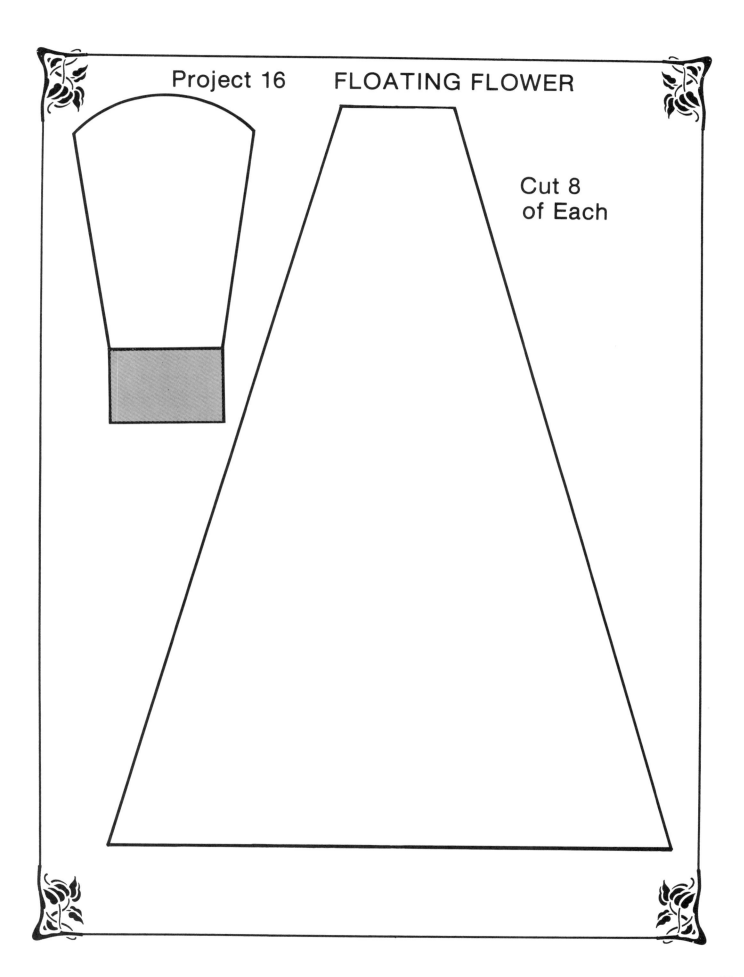

Project 16   FLOATING FLOWER

Cut 8
of Each

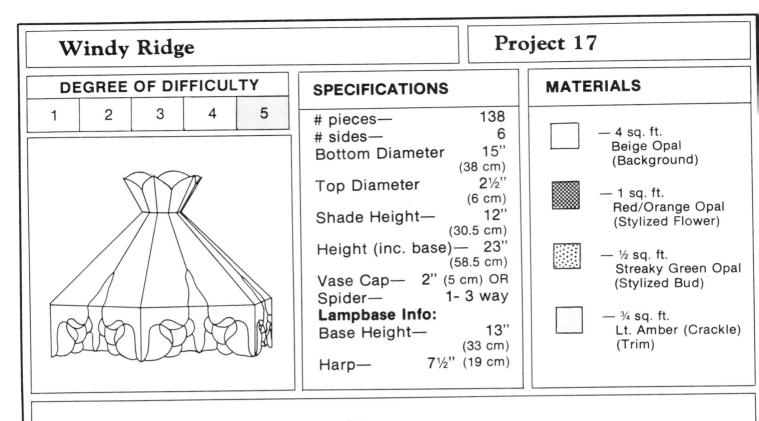

Windy Ridge

Project 17

DEGREE OF DIFFICULTY

1	2	3	4	5

SPECIFICATIONS

# pieces—	138
# sides—	6
Bottom Diameter	15"
	(38 cm)
Top Diameter	2½"
	(6 cm)
Shade Height—	12"
	(30.5 cm)
Height (inc. base)—	23"
	(58.5 cm)
Vase Cap—	2" (5 cm) OR
Spider—	1- 3 way
Lampbase Info:	
Base Height—	13"
	(33 cm)
Harp—	7½" (19 cm)

MATERIALS

- — 4 sq. ft. Beige Opal (Background)
- — 1 sq. ft. Red/Orange Opal (Stylized Flower)
- — ½ sq. ft. Streaky Green Opal (Stylized Bud)
- — ¾ sq. ft. Lt. Amber (Crackle) (Trim)

PROJECT INFORMATION:
This lampshade is suitable for both swag or lampbase.

Project 17   WINDY RIDGE

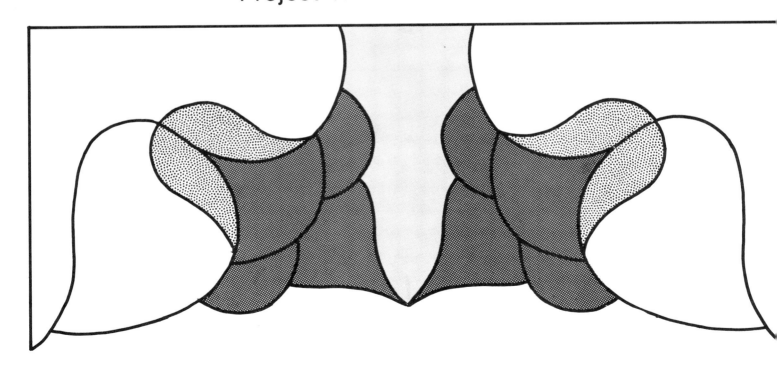

Cut 6 of Each

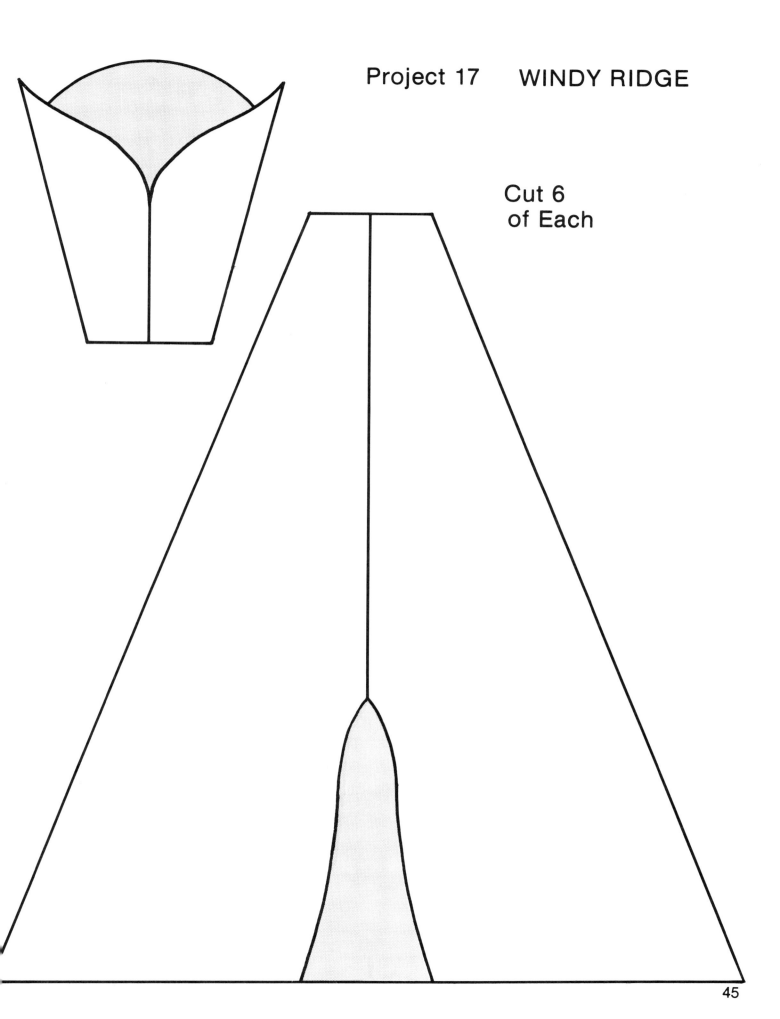

Project 17   WINDY RIDGE

Cut 6
of Each

Catharines Lamp	Project 18

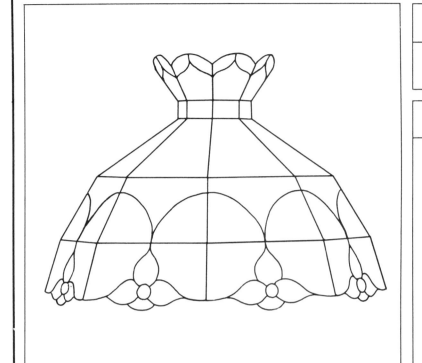

DEGREE OF DIFFICULTY

1	2	3	4	5

LAMPBASE INFO:

Does Not Apply

SPECIFICATIONS

# pieces—	120
# sides—	8
Bottom Diameter	17" (43 cm)
Top Diameter	3½" (9 cm)
Shade Height—	13¾" (35 cm)
Height (inc. base)—	N/A
Spider—	1- 4 way

MATERIALS

- 4½ sq. ft. Green in Carmel Opal (Background & crown)

- 1 sq. ft. Streaky Turquoise Cathedral (3 large flower petals & crown trim)

- 1/4 sq. ft. Amber Mirror (1 flower petal & collar)

- Nuggets or Jewels 8- ¾" (1.5 cm) Lt. Amber

PROJECT INFORMATION:
If using nuggets, size each panel to the individual nugget.

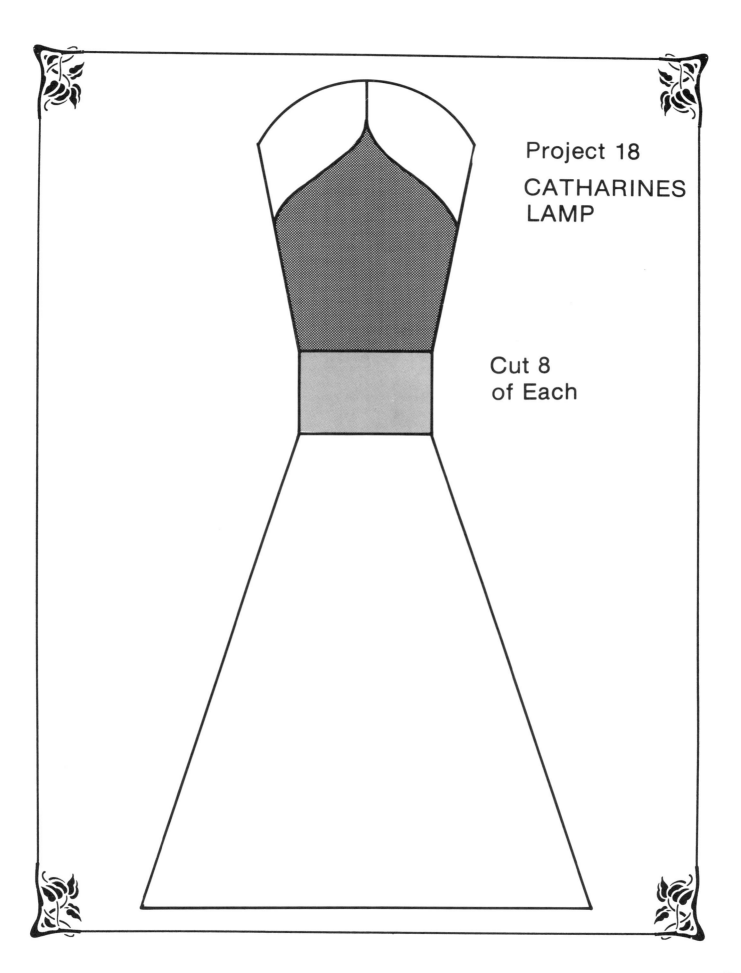

Project 18

CATHARINES
LAMP

Cut 8
of Each

Project 18   CATHARINES LAMP

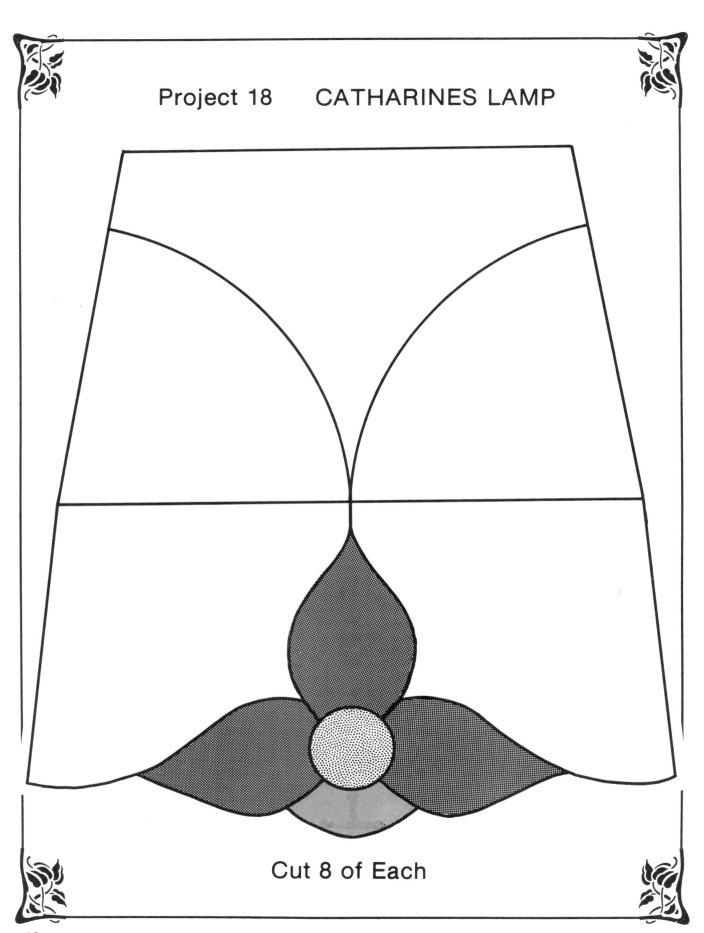

Cut 8 of Each